W9-BXE-810

EDGE BOOKS™

SPORTS RIVALRIES

OUTRAGEOUS

PRO WRESTLING
RIVALRIES

BY MATT CHANDLER

CONSULTANT: MIKE JOHNSON, WRITER (PWINSIDER.COM)

CAPSTONE PRESS
a capstone imprint

Edge Books are published by Capstone Press,
1710 Roe Crest Drive, North Mankato, Minnesota 56003
www.capstonepub.com

Library of Congress Cataloging-in-Publication Data
Cataloging-in-publication information is on file with the Library of Congress.
ISBN 978-1-4914-2028-7 (library binding)
ISBN 978-1-4914-2199-4 (eBook PDF)

Editorial Credits
Angie Kaelberer and Alesha Sullivan, editors; Ted Williams, designer;
Eric Gohl, media researcher; Tori Abraham, production specialist

Photo Credits
Alamy: ZUMA Press, Inc., 14–15; AP Images: Chris Carlson, 23 (top), Richard
Drew, 28–29, WWE/Jonathan Bachman, 19 (left); Corbis: Bettmann, 23 (bottom);
Dreamstime: Darwin Lopez, 4–5; Getty Images: Ethan Miller, cover (top), 17,
WireImage/KMazur, 21; Newscom: dpa/picture-alliance/Sebastian Kahnert, 25
(bottom), WENN Photos/BT1, 19 (right), WENN Photos/SI1, cover (bottom), 9
(bottom), 27, ZUMA Press/John Barrett, 13 (all), ZUMA Press/Leonard Ortiz, 11,
ZUMA Press/Matt Roberts, 6–7; Wikipedia: Megan Elice Meadows, 9 (top), miguel.
discart, 25 (top), Reckless Dream Photography, 1 (right), Shamsuddin Muhammad, 1
(left)

Design Elements
Shutterstock

Printed in the United States of America in Stevens Point, Wisconsin
092014   008479WZS15

Table of Contents

BLOOD, SWEAT, AND RIVALRIES 4

BIG SHOW **VS.** KANE..............................8

CM PUNK **VS.** JOHN CENA 10

JIMMY "SUPERFLY" SNUKA **VS.** "ROWDY" RODDY PIPER 12

THE ROCK **VS.** "STONE COLD" STEVE AUSTIN 14

RANDY ORTON **VS.** JOHN CENA 16

A.J. LEE **VS.** NAOMI 18

UNDERTAKER **VS.** KANE..............................20

HULK HOGAN **VS.** ANDRE THE GIANT..............................22

DOLPH ZIGGLER **VS.** KOFI KINGSTON 24

SHEAMUS **VS.** DANIEL BRYAN 26

Glossary..............................30

Read More..............................31

Internet Sites..............................31

Index..............................32

BLOOD, SWEAT, AND RIVALRIES

Some of the most brutal sports rivalries take place in pro wrestling. A U.S. arena might have 18,000 fans watching a professional World Wrestling Entertainment (WWE) wrestling match.

In 1995 Japanese wrestlers Hiro Saito and Yuji Nagata squared off in North Korea in front of 190,000 fans! Saito defeated Nagata, but it was more than a win. In wrestling the goal is to **dominate** a match. The best way to settle a rivalry is to use your **signature moves** to defeat an opponent in front of a huge crowd.

Major rivalries in pro wrestling have included some of the biggest stars in the sport, such as Kane, John Cena, and Undertaker. Rivals square off in different types of matches. "Nature Boy" Ric Flair wrestled rival Wahoo McDaniel more than 1,000 times! The two wrestled tag team matches, battle royals, and lumberjack matches.

dominate—to rule; in sports, a person dominates by winning

FROM LADDERS TO LUMBERJACKS

Imagine being locked in a steel cage with your rival. Or squaring off in a ring surrounded by fire! Wrestling is full of gimmick matches.

MATCH	DESCRIPTION
Strap Match	Wrestlers are strapped together—usually at the wrist. The strap can be used as a weapon.
Ladder Match	A prize, such as a championship belt, contract, or even cash, is placed at the top of a tall ladder. The first wrestler to reach the prize wins.
Battle Royal	As many as 30 wrestlers enter the ring at once. Wrestlers are eliminated by being thrown over the top rope until just one remains.
Steel Cage Match	A steel cage with a roof surrounds the ring. Anything is legal to use as a weapon, including the cage. To win a wrestler must pin the opponent or escape from the cage.
Lumberjack Match	The ring is surrounded by wrestlers nicknamed lumberjacks. Any time a wrestler ends up outside of the ring, the lumberjacks throw him back in. Female wrestlers take part in lumberjill matches.
Casket Match	A casket is placed outside of the ring. A wrestler must force the opponent inside of the casket and shut the lid to win.
Dark Match	These matches are held before some major pay-per-view events, such as WrestleMania. They are seen only by the fans in the arena, not on TV.
Extreme Rules Match	Wrestlers use hammers, staple guns, and other weapons. These matches are often used to settle rivalries.
Iron Man Match	This type of match has a set time limit, often 60 minutes. The wrestler with the most pinfalls at the end of the time is the winner.
"I Quit" Match	A match with no pinfalls or disqualifications. The only way to win is to get your opponent to quit.
No-Holds-Barred Match	This match has no rules. Choking, eye-gouging, punching, and other moves normally against the rules are allowed.

gimmick—a clever trick or idea used to get people's attention

pinfall—when a wrestler is pinned for a count of three; a pinfall is

Professional wrestlers have a habit of changing their minds. The Rock was locked in a bitter rivalry with Mankind in the late 1990s. The two had some of the toughest battles for the WWE World Championship title. Fans were shocked when the two enemies teamed up to challenge Undertaker and Big Show for the Tag Team title. Together they became world champions.

Superstars Big Show (left) and
Kane won an eight-man match at

Other wrestlers turn on their friends and become sworn enemies. Cody Rhodes was the last man in the ring at the 2013 Money in the Bank ladder match. In the ring Rhodes climbed the ladder to grab the briefcase hanging above it. In the case was a World Heavyweight Championship contract. But Rhodes' best friend, Damien Sandow, interfered. Sandow threw Rhodes from the ladder and stole the briefcase and contract from his friend. What do you think was the biggest wrestling rivalry of all time?

BIG SHOW VS. KANE

Sometimes the biggest rivalries are between former friends. Kane and Big Show were a top WWE tag team throughout 2005 and early 2006.

Although the two squared off dozens of times, their friendship exploded one night in California in 2006. The two giants had been locked in a slugfest when suddenly Kane took control. He slid out under the bottom rope and grabbed a steel chair. Returning to the ring, he hit Big Show with the chair 13 times. Kane was disqualified, lost the match, and a rivalry was born.

The two wrestlers met later that year in an extreme rules match. Kane couldn't be counted out or disqualified. Midway through the match, Kane seemed to have the upper hand. But Big Show was able to mount a comeback and chokeslam Kane onto a steel chair. Big Show then fell on top of Kane and covered him for the pin.

Kane and Big Show continue to battle each other. And they continue to team up for Tag Team titles. This rivalry shows no sign of slowing down.

WRESTLER SPECS

BIG SHOW

Height: 7'0" (213 cm)
Weight: 425 pounds (193 kg)
Championships Held: *World Wrestling Entertainment titles:* World Heavyweight, Tag Team, Hardcore, U.S., Intercontinental; *World Championship Wrestling title:* Champion
Signature Moves: Chokeslam, KO Punch, Colossal Clutch

KANE

Height: 7'0" (213 cm)
Weight: 323 pounds (147 kg)
Championships Held: *WWE titles:* Tag Team, World Heavyweight, Intercontinental, Hardcore; *WCW title:* Tag Team
Signature Move: Chokeslam

Big Show is ready to fight at Smack Down in 2014.

Kane holds his Tag Team championship belt during the 2012 WWE World Tour.

CM PUNK VS. JOHN CENA

John Cena is one of the toughest men to ever enter the wrestling ring. He holds more than 20 titles, including 15 **reigns** as WWE World Heavyweight Champion. No man knows that better than CM Punk. He has faced Cena many times since joining WWE in 2006.

Their biggest battle took place in February 2013 on WWE's Raw TV show. The winner would get a title match against The at WrestleMania. With the stakes high, they fought for nearly 30 minutes. CM Punk went to the top rope. He leaped from the **turnbuckle** to take down Cena with an elbow but missed. Cena took advantage of the high-flying mistake. He slammed Punk to the mat, pinning him for the win. He went on to win the WWE title from The Rock at WrestleMania.

WRESTLER SPECS

CM PUNK
Height: 6'2" (188 cm)
Weight: 218 pounds (99 kg)
Championships Held: *WWE titles:* World Heavyweight, Tag Team, Intercontinental
Signature Moves: GTS, Anaconda Vise

JOHN CENA
Height: 6'1" (185 cm)
Weight: 251 pounds (114 kg)
Championships Held: *WWE titles:* World Heavyweight, U.S., Tag Team
Signature Moves: STF, Attitude Adjustment

reign—the period of time that a person is a ruler or leader

turnbuckle—a padded area on the corner of a wrestling ring

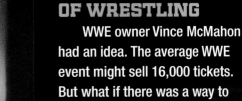

CM Punk (top) had the upper hand against Cena during Monday Night Raw in 2011.

THE SUPER BOWL OF WRESTLING

WWE owner Vince McMahon had an idea. The average WWE event might sell 16,000 tickets. But what if there was a way to have 2 million people paying to watch? In 1985 McMahon held the first WrestleMania. It changed the way fans watched pro wrestling. There were 19,000 fans inside New York's Madison Square Garden that night. But 1 million more watched on closed-circuit TV. By 1987 the event was so popular that more than 93,000 fans attended WrestleMania III in Detroit. People began to call the event the Super Bowl of wrestling.

WrestleMania often has gimmicks that set it apart from other events. Former heavyweight boxing champ Muhammad Ali served as a guest referee at the first event. Movie stars, musicians, and other pro athletes have also taken part. Even after three decades, fans can't get enough of WWE's main event.

closed-circuit— TV programming that is transmitted by satellite to many locations

11

JIMMY "SUPERFLY" SNUKA

VS.

"ROWDY" RODDY PIPER

Today it's common for wrestlers to do interviews in the ring. But in the 1980s, "Rowdy" Roddy Piper was a **pioneer**. It was during his weekly TV interview show that a major rivalry was born.

Piper's guest was Jimmy "Superfly" Snuka. Snuka's family came from the South Pacific island of Fiji. Piper mocked Snuka's Fijian heritage, throwing bananas at him and splitting open a coconut on Snuka's skull.

Snuka quickly challenged Piper to a Fijian strap match inside of the ring. The men were bound together with a long leather strap. They took turns choking each other with the strap. Snuka was able to drop Piper with a headbutt and climb to the top rope. Even though they were bound together, he launched himself across the ring and delivered his Superfly Splash. Piper was counted out, but the match wasn't over. Piper attacked Snuka, wrapped the strap around Snuka's throat, and attempted to choke him out. It took a second referee to come in and break up the two enemies.

Snuka and Piper fought many times in the 1980s. They once fought 14 matches in one month. They made peace 20 years later, but fans still consider their rivalry one of the greatest in pro wrestling.

SNUKA

RODDY PIPER

WRESTLER SPECS

JIMMY SNUKA

Height: 5'10" (178 cm)
Weight: 235 pounds (107 kg)
Championships Held: *WWE title: U.S.; Extreme Championship Wrestling title:* Heavyweight Champion
Signature Move: Superfly Splash

"ROWDY" RODDY PIPER

Height: 6'2" (188 cm)
Weight: 230 pounds (104 kg)
Championships Held: *WWE titles:* Intercontinental, World Tag Team; *WCW title:* U.S.
Signature Move: Sleeper Hold

pioneer—a person who is the first to try new things

THE ROCK
VS.
"STONE COLD" STEVE AUSTIN

Many fans consider "Stone Cold" Steve Austin and The Rock the most popular wrestlers of the late 1990s. They battled more than 100 times in their Hall of Fame careers in one of the bitterest rivalries in WWE history.

The rivalry regularly spilled outside of the ring. Austin once drove his monster truck over The Rock's new car, destroying it on live TV. He then drove the truck into the arena and attacked The Rock. Austin tossed The Rock into a grave dug in a pile of dirt near the ring.

It wasn't the last time Stone Cold would crush The Rock. They met in 1999 for a no-holds-barred match at Backlash. Austin was defending his Heavyweight title. Most of the match took place outside of the ring. The Rock hit Austin with a fire extinguisher. He smashed him through the announcer's table before tossing him back in the ring. But Austin came back to take down The Rock with the Stone Cold Stunner and kept his title.

One of the most well-known rivalries is between "Stone Cold" Steve Austin (left) and The Rock.

WRESTLER SPECS

THE ROCK

Height: 6'5" (196 cm)
Weight: 260 pounds (118 kg)
Championships Held: *WWE titles:* World Champion, Intercontinental, Tag Team; *WCW title:* Champion
Signature Move: Rock Bottom, People's Elbow

"STONE COLD" STEVE AUSTIN

Height: 6'2" (188 cm)
Weight: 252 pounds (114 kg)
Championships Held: *WWE titles:* World Champion, Intercontinental, Tag Team; *WCW titles:* U.S., Tag Team
Signature Moves: Stone Cold Stunner, DDT

RANDY ORTON
VS.
JOHN CENA

A four-month period in 2009 made Cena and Orton the most electrifying rivalry in pro wrestling. It began in June with a four-way battle for the vacant WWE title. Orton outlasted Triple H, Big Show, and his enemy Cena to capture the title. Three months later Cena choked out Orton in an "I Quit" match.

Cena held the title for just three weeks before the two locked horns in a steel cage title rematch. With no rules, Orton choked Cena and used the steel cage to punish the champion. It was a kick to the head that knocked out Cena cold and earned Orton the title.

Like Cena, Orton's reign as champion would last just three weeks. The next time they met was the biggest match of their rivalry. In a one-hour Iron Man match, Cena defeated Orton, winning six pinfalls to five.

WRESTLER SPECS

RANDY ORTON

Height: 6'5" (196 cm)
Weight: 235 pounds (107 kg)
Championships Held: *WWE titles:* World Heavyweight, Intercontinental, Tag Team
Signature Move: RKO

JOHN CENA

Height: 6'1" (185 cm)
Weight: 251 pounds (114 kg)
Championships Held: *WWE titles:* World Heavyweight, U.S., Tag Team
Signature Moves: Attitude Adjustment, STF

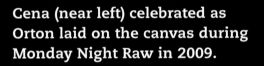

Cena (near left) celebrated as Orton laid on the canvas during Monday Night Raw in 2009.

One of the hottest rivalries in WWE pits A.J. Lee against Naomi. Both women are fast, strong, and have dangerous signature moves. In June 2013 Lee became the **Divas** Champion by defeating Kaitlyn, but Naomi was nipping at her heels.

The rivals kicked off 2014 with a series of tag team matches. Lee teamed up with Tamina Snuka, daughter of WWE legend Jimmy Snuka. Naomi partnered with Cameron. Adding two more wrestlers made the rivalry even more intense.

In March 2014 Lee and Naomi's rivalry boiled over at a lumberjill match. The two women battled as 12 other divas surrounded the ring. Their job was to keep both wrestlers from leaving the ring. But when Naomi hopped out of the ring, the lumberjills didn't move. Lee had to jump out and throw Naomi back in herself.

Halfway through the match, Lee seemed to have the upper hand. She put Naomi in a neckbreaker, but Naomi kicked out. Lee slid out of the ring, and Tamina stood to protect her. But the lumberjills attacked both Tamina and Lee and threw Lee back into the ring. Naomi quickly pinned Lee to win the match.

diva—a female wrestler

Naomi hopes to soon become a Divas Champion.

Lee proudly displays her title.

WRESTLER SPECS

A.J. LEE
Height: 5'2" (157 cm)
Championships Held: *WWE Title:* Divas Champion
Signature Moves: Black Widow, Shining Wizard

NAOMI
Height: 5'5" (165 cm)
Championships Held: None
Signature Move: Split-Legged Moonsault

UNDERTAKER
VS.
KANE

Imagine stepping into the ring to face your opponent and being surrounded by fire! That's what happened as Kane squared off against Undertaker in a 1998 **Inferno** Match. What began as a bitter rivalry exploded in a ring of flames!

With all four sides of the ring burning, there was no escape. But Undertaker found a way out. After throwing Kane through the wall of fire, he did the unthinkable. He leaped over the flames, landing on Kane and falling to the arena floor. After attacking Kane's manager, Paul Bearer, Undertaker forced Kane into the flames. Kane ran to the locker room—with his arm on fire!

Like any good rivalry, this one had a long history. Months earlier Kane interfered in a casket match between Undertaker and WWE Champion Shawn Michaels. After clearing the ring, Kane chokeslammed Undertaker into the casket. He locked Undertaker inside. With Paul Bearer's help, he lit the casket on fire! When emergency workers put out the fire, the casket was empty. Undertaker had escaped. But he would return to seek revenge on Kane.

Any type of friendship between Undertaker (left) and Kane went up in smoke.

WRESTLER SPECS

UNDERTAKER

Height: 6'10" (208 cm)
Weight: 299 pounds (136 kg)
Championships Held: WWE titles: World Heavyweight, Tag Team, Hardcore; WCW title: Tag Team
Signature Moves: Chokeslam, Tombstone Piledriver, Last Ride

KANE

Height: 7'0" (213 cm)
Weight: 323 pounds (147 kg)
Championships Held: WWE titles: Tag Team, World Heavyweight, Intercontinental, Hardcore; WCW title: Tag Team
Signature Move: Chokeslam

HULK HOGAN
VS.
ANDRE THE GIANT

As World Heavyweight Champion Hulk Hogan entered the ring, 93,173 fans rose to their feet. Hogan was wrestling in the main event of 1987, WrestleMania III. In the ring stood his challenger, Andre the Giant. Hogan was there not only to defend his title but also to settle a score. Andre had turned **heel**. His new manager, Bobby "The Brain" Heenan, convinced him he had to beat Hogan. Andre had never lost a match, but Hogan was still considered the best. Andre wanted to change that.

Though Hulk was a crowd favorite, Andre used his massive size to pummel the champ early. It looked as though Hogan's reign at the top would end.

But Hogan never gave up. With the crowd behind him, he began to attack Andre. After wearing him down, Hogan did two things no man had ever done. He scoop-slammed the 520-pound (236-kg) Giant and then pinned him for the win. The Giant's unbeaten streak was over, and a rivalry was born.

Andre got his revenge in a rematch in February 1988. He defeated Hogan to capture his first World Heavyweight title. But then he gave the championship belt to Ted DiBiase. WWE officials said that deal was against the rules. A 14-wrestler match at WrestleMania IV would determine the champion. At WrestleMania Hogan and Andre hit each other with a steel chair, resulting in a double disqualification.

Hogan and Andre wrestled for the last time at SummerSlam in 1988. It was a tag team match where Hogan and Randy Savage defeated Andre and Ted DiBiase. Three years later, health problems forced Andre to retire from wrestling. He died in 1993.

heel—a wrestler who acts as a villain in the ring

Ripping off his shirt is one of Hogan's pre-match moves.

At over 7 feet (213 cm) tall, Andre was a giant.

WRESTLER SPECS

HULK HOGAN

Height: 6'7" (201 cm)
Weight: 302 pounds (137 kg)
Championships Held: *WWE titles:* World Heavyweight Champion, Tag Team; *WCW title:* World Champion
Signature Move: Leg Drop

ANDRE THE GIANT

Height: 7'4" (224 cm)
Weight: 520 pounds (236 kg)
Championships Held: *WWE titles:* World Heavyweight Champion, Tag Team
Signature Move: Sitdown Splash

DOLPH ZIGGLER
VS.
KOFI KINGSTON

When Dolph Ziggler and Kofi Kingston step into
the ring, fans know they are in for a fast-paced match.
Kingston is known for flying kicks, dives from the ropes,
and flying elbows. Ziggler is one of the few men who can
match him move for move.

The rivalry peaked at a match in January 2011.
Intercontinental Champion Ziggler had defended the title
five consecutive nights against Kingston to end 2010. But
Kingston's luck was about to change. After wearing the
champion down, Kofi climbed to the top rope. He flew
across the ring and stunned Ziggler with a cross body
block. Kingston hooked one of Ziggler's legs and secured
the win.

Instead of celebrating Kingston was forced to defend
his title immediately. With no time to rest, it looked as
though Kingston's championship reign might be short.
Then Kingston delivered a Trouble in Paradise flying spin
kick to Ziggler's head. Ziggler was out cold, and Kingston
earned the easy pin.

Kingston pumped up the crowd during the 2012 Wrestlemania Tour.

WRESTLER SPECS

DOLPH ZIGGLER

Height: 6'0" (183 cm)
Weight: 213 pounds (97 kg)
Championships Held: *WWE titles:* Intercontinental, World Heavyweight, U.S.
Signature Move: Zig Zag

KOFI KINGSTON

Height: 6'0" (183 cm)
Weight: 212 pounds (96 kg)
Championships Held: *WWE titles:* Intercontinental, U.S, Tag Team
Signature Move: Trouble in Paradise

SHEAMUS
VS.
DANIEL BRYAN

Sheamus joined WWE in 2006, and Daniel Bryan entered the ring in 2010. But they quickly became fan favorites and rivals. In 2011 WrestleMania featured U.S. Champion Sheamus and Bryan in a lumberjack-style dark match. When Bryan tossed Sheamus from the ring, the lumberjacks attacked. Bryan responded by diving over the top rope to deliver a blow to Sheamus. Soon it was an all-out war as 20 men battled outside of the ring. The referee stopped the match, and Sheamus escaped with his title.

But the biggest match in this rivalry may be one in which Bryan wasn't even scheduled to wrestle. In April 2012 Sheamus was set to defend his title against Mark Henry on Raw. At the last minute, Bryan was announced as the guest referee. Bryan distracted Sheamus throughout the match. He finally got him to turn his back. Henry delivered the finishing blow. Bryan hit the mat and delivered a lightning-fast three-count.

Bryan then stripped off his referee shirt and beat Sheamus in the center of the ring. Bryan locked the champion into his signature Yes! Headlock and left him face down in the ring.

Sheamus (left) clung to his World Heavyweight title in an epic fight against Bryan (right) during Smack Down in 2012.

WRESTLER SPECS

SHEAMUS

Height: 6'4" (193 cm)
Weight: 267 pounds (121 kg)
Championships Held: *WWE titles:* U.S., World Heavyweight
Signature Moves: Brogue Kick, Cloverleaf, Irish Curse Backbreaker

DANIEL BRYAN

Height: 5'10" (178 cm)
Weight: 210 pounds (95 kg)
Championships Held: *WWE titles:* Tag Team, World Heavyweight, U.S.
Signature Move: Yes! Headlock

27

NO SIGNS OF SLOWING DOWN

Once they step inside the ring, professional wrestlers have no true friends. Only the strongest, toughest wrestlers become champions. Managers will turn on their own wrestlers to win a title. Tag team partners will attack each other. There is no loyalty. It's that approach that has created some of the most exciting matchups in the history of sports.

But the biggest rivalries in wrestling are created by the fans. They pick their favorites and boo the ones they dislike. The energy in an arena is what fuels the greatest rivalries in professional wrestling.

Hulk Hogan (right) and Andre the Giant faced each other in and out of the ring.

Glossary

closed-circuit (KLOHZD-SUHR-kuht)—TV programming that is transmitted by satellite to many locations

disqualify (dis-KWAHL-uh-fy)—to prevent someone from taking part in or winning an activity; athletes can be disqualified for breaking the rules of their sport

diva (DEE-vuh)—a female wrestler

dominate (DAH-muh-nayt)—to rule; in sports, a person dominates by winning much more than anyone else

gimmick (GIM-ik)—a clever trick or idea used to get people's attention

heel (HEEL)—a wrestler who acts as a villain in the ring

inferno (in-FUHR-noh)—an intense fire

lumberjack (LUHM-bur-jak)—in wrestling, a male wrestler who stands outside of the ring during a lumberjack match

pinfall (pin-FAWL)—when a wrestler is pinned for a count of three; a pinfall is also called a fall

pioneer (pye-o-NEER)—a person who is the first to try new things

reign (RAYN)—the period of time that a person is a ruler or leader

signature move (SIG-nuh-chur MOOV)—the move for which a wrestler is best known; this move is also called a finishing move

turnbuckle (TURN-buh-kuhl)—a padded area on the corner of a wrestling ring

Read More

Kaelberer, Angie Peterson. *The Fabulous, Freaky, Unusual History of Pro Wrestling.* Unusual Histories. Mankato, Minn.: Capstone Press, 2011.

Price, Sean. *The Kids' Guide to Pro Wrestling.* Kids' Guides. Mankato, Minn.: Capstone Press, 2012.

West, Tracey. *Brothers of Destruction.* New York: Grosset & Dunlap, 2011.

Internet Sites

FactHound offers a safe, fun way to find Internet sites related to this book. All of the sites on FactHound have been researched by our staff.

Here's all you do:

Visit *www.facthound.com*

Type in this code: 9781491420287

Super-cool stuff!

Check out projects, games and lots more at
www.capstonekids.com

Index

Ali, Muhammad, 11
Andre the Giant, 22, 23, 29
Austin, "Stone Cold" Steve, 14, 15

Big Show, 6, 8, 9, 16
Bryan, Daniel, 26, 27

Cena, John, 4, 10, 11, 16, 17
chokeslam, 8, 20
CM Punk, 10, 11

DiBiase, Ted, 22
Divas Champion, 18, 19

Flair, "Nature Boy" Ric, 4

Heenan, Bobby "The Brain," 22
Henry, Mark, 26
Hogan, Hulk, 22, 23, 29

Kaitlyn, 18
Kane, 4, 6, 8, 9, 20, 21
Kingston, Kofi, 24, 25

Lee, A.J., 18, 19

McDaniel, Wahoo, 4
McMahon, Vince, 11
Michaels, Shawn, 20

Nagata, Yuji, 4
Naomi, 18, 19

Orton, Randy, 16, 17

Piper, "Rowdy" Roddy, 12, 13

Rhodes, Cody, 7

Saito, Hiro, 4
Sandow, Damien, 7
Savage, Randy, 22
Sheamus, 26, 27
Snuka, Jimmy "Superfly," 12, 13, 18
Snuka, Tamina, 18
SummerSlam, 22

tag team, 4, 6, 8, 9, 18, 22, 28
The Rock, 6, 10, 14, 15
Triple H, 16

Undertaker, 4, 6, 20, 21

World Heavyweight Champion, 7, 10, 14, 22, 27
World Wrestling Entertainment (WWE), 4, 6, 8, 9, 10, 11, 14, 16, 18, 20, 22, 26
WrestleMania, 5, 6, 10, 11, 22, 25, 26

Ziggler, Dolph, 24, 25